D0816558

Massive Machines

By Bob Woods

The Child's World®

www.childsworld.com

Published in the United States of America by The Child's World®
1980 Lookout Drive • Mankato, MN 56003-1705
800-599-READ • www.childsworld.com

ACKNOWLEDGMENTS

The Child's World® : Mary Berendes, Publishing Director

Produced by Shoreline Publishing Group LLC
President / Editorial Director: James Buckley, Jr.
Designer: Tom Carling, carlingdesign.com
Cover Design: Slimfilms

Photo Credits
Cover–Courtesy Robbins Co. (main); Courtesy Komatsu (insets)
Interior–Corbis: 5, 11, 14, 21; John Deere & Company, Moline, Ill.:
9, 24; Dreamstime.com: 18, 19; Courtesy Kalamarind: 6; Courtesy
Komatsu: 13, 22; Courtesy Robbins Co.: 26; SpaceStock: 17.

LIBRARY OF CONGRESS CATALOG-IN-PUBLICATION DATA

Woods, Bob.
  Massive machines / by Bob Woods.
     p. cm. — (Reading rocks!)
  Includes index.
  ISBN-13: 978-1-59296-858-9 (library bound : alk. paper)
  ISBN-10: 1-59296-858-9 (library bound : alk. paper)
 1. Construction equipment—Juvenile literature. I. Title. II.
Series.

 TH900W66 2007
 629.225—dc22

                              2007011417

CONTENTS

4 CHAPTER 1
Heavy Lifters

12 CHAPTER 2
Humongous
Haulers

22 CHAPTER 3
Enormous
Earth-Movers

30 GLOSSARY

31 FIND OUT MORE

32 INDEX

HEAVY
Lifters

Massive machines are needed for all sorts of really big jobs. Whether building a 50-story skyscraper or digging a super-long tunnel, busy work crews use lots of huge, amazing equipment.

A gigantic ring crane can lift 2,500 tons—that's 5 million pounds (2.2 million kg)! It can lift heavy building materials nearly 350 feet (107 m) into the air. The crane has a super-long steel arm, called a **boom**, that bends up and down—just as your arm does.

The driver of a ring crane sits in a cab. In this picture, the cab is the dark-colored box.

Thick, strong cables are attached to each load. Then the crane roars into action, and the load rises!

Ring cranes are used to erect tall buildings, bridges, and other structures that soar high in the sky.

The straddle carrier rolls over the top of a container, then lifts it.

When the job calls for moving ultra-heavy loads, such as stacks of lumber or giant boxes, workers use a **straddle** carrier. These wheeled machines pick up and carry **cargo.** The cargo is then loaded onto ships, airplanes, railroad cars, and trucks for delivery all over the world.

Cargo is anything (other than people) that is carried on a ship, train, truck, airplane, or car.

Here's how a straddle carrier works: imagine you're standing over a box of wooden blocks with your legs apart. (You're "straddling" the blocks.) You bend down, pick up as many blocks as you can, and slowly walk them over to the case. Now, lower them into the case. Job well done! Of course, straddle carriers lift weights thousands of times heavier than a box of blocks!

Green forests cover vast areas of the Earth. Sometimes parts of a forest need to be cleared to make way for new buildings or roads. Trees are also chopped down to make lumber used for houses, furniture, toys, and even the paper this book is printed on.

To save trees, more and more books are printed on recycled paper. One out of every ten pounds of paper used to make this book came from recycled materials.

After tall trees are sawed down, the long **timbers** must be picked up and carried away. They're much too heavy for people to lift, so it's a job for a grapple skidder. A grapple is a giant claw that can scoop up several thick timbers at a time. A skidder is the tough, four-wheeled vehicle to which the grapple is attached. Firmly gripping the mighty logs, the grapple skidder hauls them through the dense forest. Then it loads all the timbers onto a waiting flatbed truck. The truck then delivers the timbers to a saw mill.

The large yellow fingers at the front of this machine grab the logs.

Fire trucks are certainly popular with many kids. They're also hard-working, great-looking machines. They help brave firefighters do very important—and sometimes dangerous—work in big cities and small towns everywhere.

Some fire trucks just carry long hoses and pump water from a **hydrant** to put out a blaze.

Fighting Mine Fires

The Queensland Mines Rescue Service in Australia has what it calls "the world's biggest mobile fire **extinguisher**." It's used to put out underground fires in coal mines. The extinguisher has a military jet engine that shoots a white mist at speeds of about 55 mph (89 kph). The mist is forced deep into the mine to extinguish the fire. It's mounted on a special 45-foot (14-m) flatbed truck.

A hose runs the length of the ladder, too. Firefighters can use the hose to shoot water from the top of the ladder.

The most marvelous kind of fire truck is the hook and ladder. It has one enormous ladder on its top. It **extends** like a telescope. Firefighters then climb to reach flames or trapped people. The ladder goes higher than 100 feet (30 m).

2

HUMONGOUS Haulers

Dump trucks are definitely on the Massive Machines All-Star Team. No amount of dirt, sand, rock, metal, or other material is too much for these workhorses.

Dump trucks tip up and backwards, a door in back opens, and the load dumps out. Then the truck roars off to pick up another load.

The mightiest type of dump truck is the giant, off-road dump truck. It's used by crews building new highways and mines. This big bruiser stands about 24 feet (7 m) tall—as high as a two-story building. It weighs nearly 224 tons (203,000 kg). Each of its six tires is twice as tall as the average worker. Powered by a 3,650-**horsepower** engine, this type of truck can carry a load of more than 180 tons (163,000 kg).

Follow the ladders to find out how the driver reaches the wheel, high above the ground.

Check out the "tiny" truck at the bottom center to see just how huge this transporter really is.

Have you ever seen the space shuttle lift off? It's attached to three huge rockets to blast it into space. But did you ever wonder how NASA moves the shuttle and the rockets to the launchpad? That's the unique job of what NASA calls the crawler-transporter.

This rig is big! Standing on four double-tracked "feet," the transporter is 131 feet (40 m) long and 114 feet (35 m) wide. That's about the size of half a football field! The crawler-transporter is 26 feet (8 m) tall and weighs 5.5 million pounds (2.5 million kg).

Even with 16 motors, the crawler-transporter goes only 1 mile (1.6 km) per hour. So the journey from the building where NASA keeps the shuttle to the launchpad takes at least five hours. You can probably crawl faster than that!

Bt the end of 2006, 116 space shuttle missions had been launched. The first was *Columbia*, which took off on April 12, 1981.

The crawler-transporter is certainly a huge machine. But the space shuttle that it carries is pretty gigantic itself. Every space shuttle has huge fuel tanks and rockets (see picture). When standing on end, the shuttle and tanks are 184 feet (56 m) high!

The shuttle's main "orbiter" section is 122 feet (37 m) long and stands 57 feet (17 m) tall. Its wings, used to help it land like an airplane, are 78 feet (24 m) wide. The entire spaceship is about as big as a large passenger airplane.

Since 1981, five space shuttles have been built for use by astronauts from around the world.

The giant orange and white tubes are fuel tanks. When they're empty, the white tanks fall back into the sea to be reused later. The orange tank burns up as it falls back to Earth.

Flatbed trailers must be pulled by powerful truck "cabs" like this one.

A flatbed is not a bed you sleep on—although hundreds of mattresses could be stacked on top of one flatbed truck.

Think of a flatbed truck as a long table on wheels. Most flatbeds are trailers. That means they don't have an engine, so they have to be pulled behind a truck. Flatbed trailers carry all kinds of heavy objects, including cars, logs, and houses.

Several flatbeds can be linked together behind a cab engine. Then they form a sort of train that runs on the road instead of rails. These road trains are used to transport very long storage tanks, rockets, construction cranes, and other lengthy loads.

Longest Road Train

Australia has many long, flat roads across its vast deserts. Road trains are often used to haul goods. In 2006, a single truck pulled 104 flatbeds behind it to form such a road train. The parade of containers set a Guinness World Record, stretching almost a mile (1.6 km)!

Farmers use lots of different machines. Some are small, such as a pickup truck or a tractor. One massive farm machine is the harvester. It's used to pick tons of corn, cotton, and other **crops**.

"Crops" is a short word that covers a lot of ground. Just about any products that people grow for food or to use in other ways can be called crops.

The cotton harvester is an amazing machine that's made life much easier for cotton farmers. One hundred years ago, cotton had to be picked by hand. Today that **backbreaking** job, which required many people, is done by one person driving a harvester.

Cotton plants grow in long rows that cover huge fields. When the cotton is ripe, the harvester moves through the field on wheels. It's wide enough to pick six rows at a time. It scoops up the puffy cotton **bolls** and shoots them into a giant basket on the harvester.

This team of harvesters can clear an enormous field in very little time.

3

ENORMOUS EARTH-
Movers

A bulldozer is a powerful earth-mover. With its wide, curved blade in front, it pushes heavy loads of dirt, sand, rock, and whatever else needs pushing around. It moves on metal tracks that dig into the ground.

A bulldozer doesn't go fast, but it can go almost anywhere on land. Its tracks let it climb up rugged hills, through thick forests, or over ice and snow. The bulldozer pushes away anything in its path.

OPPOSITE PAGE
Look how big this bulldozer is compared to the man standing in front of it!

The bulldozer is a hardworking machine on any construction job. It helps clear land for new houses and roads that are being built. Bulldozers can also be found at work in mines, on farms, and in forests.

You've heard of first-graders and second-graders. Well, meet an earth-grader. When it's time to build a brand-new road or highway, this powerful machine roars to the head of the class.

Every road has to be flat. Even if it has curves or hills, the road should

This earth-grader has six wheels. It can easily plow through heavy dirt, sand, and rocks.

DEERE

872

not be rough and bumpy. So the main job of the earth-grader is to make the ground flat or level. Then the road is ready to be paved with **asphalt**.

The most important part of the earth-grader is its long, curved blade. Think of it as a curved shovel. The blade pushes dirt, sand, or pebbles to make a flat surface. Imagine running the edge of your pointer finger across a rough pile of sand. Your finger pushes the sand forward as it flattens the pile. That's how an earth-grader works.

Earth-movers help build a lot of road. The U.S. Interstate Highway System connects the lower 48 U.S. states. In 2004, all those highways added up to a total of 46,837 miles (75,377 km).

The giant white wheel at the front of this tunnel borer spins at high speeds and drills through the ground to make a tunnel.

To make a perfectly round hole in a piece of wood, a carpenter uses an electric drill. To make a giant hole in the ground, you'd need a giant drill. Meet the tunnel borer! This mighty machine is nearly as long as a football field and as tall as a four-story building. Like a monstrous mechanical earthworm, a tunnel borer drills huge, perfectly round holes through miles of rock and dirt.

Tunnels are dug under cities to build subways. Other tunnels go under rivers for cars and trucks. Highway and railroad tunnels might go through mountains.

To make all these tunnels, the tunnel borer has a giant wheel covered with strong metal teeth. The wheel spins and grinds through soil. The borer is pushed forward by powerful engines.

The 33-Mile Tube

The longest railroad tunnel in the world is in Japan. The Seikan Tunnel connects the islands of Honshu and Hokkaido. It's 33.5 miles (54 km) long. Digging began in 1971 and the tunnel finally opened in 1988. It cost $3.6 billion to build. In some parts, the rock was too hard—even for a mighty tunnel borer. So workers had to blast through with dynamite.

More than half of the electricity used in the United States is created by burning coal. Ninety percent of all the coal mined is used for this purpose.

So what's the most massive of all the massive machines? The Bagger 288, built in Germany, is the world's largest and heaviest land vehicle. It's an **excavator** which is a digging machine that can rip through rock, dirt, and other hard surfaces. The Bagger 288 is mostly used to dig for coal.

This biggest-rig-of-all stands about 315 feet (96 m) high and stretches nearly 790 feet (241 m) in length.

It digs with a spinning, 71-foot (22-m) wheel. The wheel has 18 big buckets that scoop up soil and rock. In one day, the Bagger 288 can chew through an area the size of a football field, going nearly 100 feet (30 m) deep. It can dig 240,000 tons (218 million kg!) of coal in just one day's work.

Digging, lifting, hauling, flying, or tunneling—massive machines do all that and more!

The Bagger 288 digs out coal at one end and spits it out at the other (far left).

GLOSSARY

asphalt a mixture of tar and gravel that is poured out to form roads

backbreaking very tiring, difficult work

bolls fluffy balls on a cotton plant that are spun into cotton thread

boom the long arm on a crane that raises and lowers loads

cargo goods that are carried by airplanes, ships, or trains

crops plants that are grown to be used by people or animals

excavator a machine that digs into the ground

extends makes longer

extinguisher a tool that puts out fires with foam or chemicals

horsepower a measurement of an engine's power

hydrant a metal pipe that provides water for firefighters' hoses

straddle to stand with one leg on either side of something

timbers trees after they are cut down

FIND OUT MORE

BOOKS

The Big Dig: Reshaping an American City
by Peter Vanderwarker (Little Brown, 2001)
See how giant machines—and hard-working people—created an enormous project in Boston.

Space Shuttle
by Mark Bergin and David Salariya (Franklin Watts, 1999)
This book features a closer look at how the space shuttle is built and how it operates in space.

Trucks: Pickups to Big Rigs
by Adrianna Morganelli (Crabtree Publishing, 2007)
Read about monster trucks, construction vehicles, and more in this photo-filled book.

WEB SITES

Visit our Web page for lots of links about massive machines: www.childsworld.com/links

Note to Parents, Teachers, and Librarians: We routinely check our Web links to make sure they're safe, active sites—so encourage your readers to check them out!

INDEX

Australia, 10

Bagger 288, 28-29

bulldozer, 23

Columbia, 15

crawler-transporter, 15, 16

dump trucks, 12-13

earth-graders, 24-25

fire trucks, 10-11

flatbed truck, 9, 10, 18-19

Germany, 28

grapple skidder, 8-9

harvesters, 20-21

hook and ladder, 11

Japan, 27

NASA, 15, 16

Queensland Mines Rescue Service, 10

ring crane, 4-5

road train, 19

Seikan Tunnel, 27

space shuttle, 14-15, 16-17

straddle carrier, 7

tunnel borer, 26-27

U.S. Interstate Highway System, 25

BOB WOODS has written many books about cars, motorcycles, and other cool machines, along with books about NASCAR and other sports. He is a longtime magazine writer and editor who lives in Connecticut.